BOOKS BY HOWARD MOSS

A Swimmer in the Air
The Toy Fair
The Wound and the Weather

A SWIMMER IN THE AIR

A SWIMMER IN THE AIR

POEMS
by
HOWARD MOSS

CHARLES SCRIBNER'S SONS
NEW YORK

For G. P.

ACKNOWLEDGMENTS

The following poems were first published in *The New Yorker*: A SUMMER GONE, SMALL ELEGY, THE TORTOISE-SHELL LORGNETTE, THE GIFT TO BE SIMPLE, UNDERWOOD, LOCAL PLACES, A BOX AT THE OPERA, RAIN, and A WINTER COME.

Other poems first appeared in *The Hudson Review, Poetry, Harper's Bazaar, The Times Literary Supplement* (London), *Modern Writing, The Chicago Review, The New Republic, The Nation, Poetry London-New York, Commentary* and *The Western Review*, and in the anthologies, *The New Pocket Anthology of American Verse, Imagination's Other Place, The Silver Treasury of Light Verse*.

Contents

I

A SUMMER GONE

(For Mildred Wood)

I

The brilliant seaside glitters its farewell
To bathers who pack up their stripes and go
Home from all the cottages that water built;
Deserted on deserted dunes, those stilts
Of slipshod timber watch the sun run out
Among their crooked legs to meet the sea.
The windows, darker as the days go by,
Drink in the liquor of the autumn light.

II

The spiral shells, now empty of their hosts
That noiselessly would hunt the sands at night,
Are not more empty than a house I know
Whose windows, boarded up, are black with dark.
The inner and the outer night converge

On blind astronomers who used to search
The summer sky for stars. The stars that fall,
In quick succession, are not seen at all.

III

Say there was a tree that once you loved
That storms drilled downward. It was but a sign
Of how the seasons wither in a man.
Its leaves will spring into your winter mind,
Until your mind's a winter lacking spring,
Until your mind is nothing but a spring
That feeds the network of another tree
That storms will work at till the roots are free.

IV

Intrinsic as the crickets are to night,
The summer night is music made by them.
Uncritical, we listen to their themes.
The little orchestras that lure the stars
Down, down from fiery perimeters
Until we seem to touch them with our hands,
Have chirped into a silence. Where are they
Who plucked the hours of our sleep away?

V

Is it love that makes our summers shine?
Ideas of love, I mean. The naked limbs:
Bronze gears that cut the bluest sky to shreds
By running past reclining, sandy heads?
Sweet breasts that hold the very heart of love?
All shapely weights that we are mad to love?
Those beautiful outsides, those thin-skinned maps
Are part of love. Or all of it, perhaps.

VI

The insects scatter on their flimsy wings
And disappear. Sometimes one finds a trace
Of one, and sees a wingless carapace
Erosion has a mind to sculpture in.
Such tiny fans, fantastic skins are they,
One cannot hold them in the hand. The wind
Will bear, invisible upon the air,
Those cenotaphs to nothingness away.

VII

If you have listened to a summer rain,
You cannot think it will not come again:
Dead thunder that put tonnage in a drum,
Light rummaging to crack its fork on sky;
If, sleeping on a sun porch rinsed by rain
(A vine of morning-glories climbed the pane
Outside), you plumbed the very depths of sleep,
You know the silences through which sound seeps.

VIII

Sea purses lie on the September beach,
Miniature, old-fashioned sleds of black,
The runners clawlike, paired parentheses.
These are egg cases of the skate or shark,
And if they ever held their dangerous young,
Indented by the hand, like dry seaweed,
The horny little shapes hold nothing now.
Each is an artifact that you can hold.

IX

There is a time when feeling knows two things:
The dead bird lying, and the whir of wings.
Those travellers who beat the upper air
Have clarities in mind—a south somewhere,
Where clouds are higher and the sea more blue.
Diviners of the tropics have to go
Where summer is still spoken. Autumn wings
Time the distances between two things.

X

Sad fall, a thousand dyings color you:
The sunburnt skin of leaves. Of love, the view
To take is but another wintry one,
To wait for the new nestings of the sun.
Happy for the leaves that make us sad,
We walk across your fields of richest plaid,
Grateful for the view. We'll have, someday,
That other weather that we salt away.

II

THE FALLS OF LOVE

I

I know so many stories marred by love,
Tales told by bitter voices in the dark:
Those who stand before the open window
Afraid to see their hands that might let go;
And other hands that count departed loves,
Ten icicles inside a pair of gloves.

II

What faces tell its crooked narrative
Make everywhere their small appearances:
Dried flags of warning that commemorate
A feast that failed, or fasts that failure fed;
Or worse, young faces that too soon reveal
How eyes may witness what they cannot feel.

III

Only lovers rest in summer's grove,
Warm in the hollow belly of the hill.
They feel the lizard's slowness, see the sea
The mother of desire, and become the tree
They shelter under. As those leaves of skin
Burn, they burn to say: Love, stay, till autumn.

IV

A winter comes where love will never live:
In darkened windows, shadowed heads receive
Night sounds that hold affection in their strings,
And harp on the harpings of themselves to give
Cold strumming warm illusion, and to stir
False, five-fold music in the listener.

V

A body without love is in its grave.
There is a still life that all sleepers dread
That only love can motion from the dead.

Though he walk upright where green grasses wave,
He wears a little earth upon his head
Who shuns the marriage for the single bed.

VI

They rise up shining who have love to give;
Who give love freely may all things receive.
Though streams they cross can never be the same,
They know the waters of the earth are one;
They see the waking face inside the dream
Who know the variations are the theme.

VII

I know so many stories marred by love,
What faces tell its crooked narrative.
Only lovers rest in summer's grove;
A winter comes where love will never live.
A body without love is in its grave—
They rise up shining who have love to give.

THE GIFT TO BE SIMPLE

Breathing something German at the end,
Which no one understood, he died, a friend,
   Or so he meant to be, to all of us.
   Only the stars defined his radius;
His life, restricted to a wooden house,
Was in his head. He saw a fledgling fall.
   Two times he tried to nest it, but it fell
   Once more, and died; he wandered home again—
   We save so plain a story for great men.
     An angel in ill-fitting sweaters,
     Writing children naïve letters,
   A violin player lacking vanities,
   A giant wit among the homilies—
We have no parallel to that immense
       Intelligence.

But if he were remembered for the Bomb,
As some may well remember him, such a tomb,
   For one who hated violence and ceremony
   Equally, would be a wasted irony.

[14]

He flew to formal heavens from his perch,
A scientist become his own research,
   And even if the flames were never gold
   That lapped his body to an ash gone cold,
   Even if his death no trumpets tolled,
      There is enough of myth inside the truth
      To make a monument to fit him with;
   And since the universe is in a jar,
There is no weeping where his heavens are,
And I would remember, now the world is less,
      His gentleness.

THOSE WHO CANNOT ARE CONDEMNED

"Those who cannot remember the past
are condemned to repeat it."
SANTAYANA

Shipwrecked in daylight and docked in dark,
The blindman lacks a mirror in each eye,
But from the ticking clock and the crowing cock
He maps, in the dark, a visionary sky.
Seeing all the planets and the stars plain
Inside his head, and sensing the terrain,
He needs no walking stick to walk again.

No repetitions dawn, no dark comes back,
Distinguishing the twilight from the sun,
And though his world is uniformly black,
He sees realities in unison.
And there are those who see far less than he
By seeing more, and choose a twisted key
To lock themselves from their necessity.

For memory distorts the ghosts that ply
The glassy lightness of their mirrors; they
Tempt the senses to a kind of play
In which the characters are scenery;
No audience awaits the end but one
Who stares at nothing, and will blindly run
Equally from darkness as from sun.

Some closet all their dead behind one door
And mourn the apparitions they have sown
And rattle on the knob while they implore
Freedom from a jail, which is their own.
Some ageless children murder dreams they gave
Away too soon, and harpies in the grave
Make merrier the birth-rites while they rave.

And some invent a calendar that time
Has never witnessed, drawing on the air
Impossible mythologies, and some
Drag through the Odysseys of their despair,
And locked up, finally, in self-made doom,
Wander in their dark from room to room,
Unweaving threads of their unsubtle loom.

And some rehearse a future that the world
Will weed out carelessly: uprooted trees
Flung in a field where winter wind has furled
Along the bough of hope its icicles;
And others, in great pain, will travel far
For false translations of the way they were;
And some will die not knowing who they are.

A MARRIAGE

O hardly out of hate,
He flew down flights of stairs
   To where she lay;
   Too tender to berate
     His long delay,
   She fell in love with flight.

He fell in love with her,
Who'd counted all the stares
   That marked his way.
   A tardy traveller
     In love with time,
   He heard the clocks whir.

She heard the cocks wake
Pastel and country towns.
   He loved the city,
   Dangerous as a snake,
     In love with him.
   She heard his heart break.

He saw her broken eyes
Too many years too late
To make them whole;
He found, to his surprise,
It was himself
Who dammed those pretty eyes.

She pitied pity. Wise
Too late, she thought she'd take
To dressing up
In any old disguise
To keep from him
Their happiness of lies.

Though happy for a time,
He came to know too soon
The cost of tears
Unshed. He aped her crime
For years. For years,
They lived a double shame.

And they could never give
Enough to get away
    From where they hid,
    And both took to the grave
        The harm they did,
    Their necessary love.

HORROR MOVIE

Dr. Unlikely, we love you so,
You who made the double-headed rabbits grow
From a single hare. Mutation's friend,
Who could have prophecied the end
When the Spider Woman deftly snared the fly
And the monsters strangled in a monstrous kiss
And somebody hissed, "You'll hang for this!"?

Dear Dracula, sleeping on your native soil,
(Any other kind makes him spoil),
How we clapped when you broke the French door
  down
And surprised the bride in the overwrought bed.
Perfectly dressed for lunar research,
Your evening cape added much,
Though the bride, inexplicably dressed in furs,
Was a study in jaded jugulars.

Poor, tortured Leopard Man, you changed your spots
In the debauched village of the Pin-Head Tots;

How we wrung our hands, how we wept
When the eighteenth murder proved inept,
And, caught in the Phosphorous Cave of Sea,
Dangling the last of synthetic flesh,
You said, "There's something wrong with me."

The Wolf Man knew when he prowled at dawn,
Beginnings spin a web where endings spawn.
The bat who lived on shaving cream,
A household pet of Dr. Dream,
Unfortunately, maddened by the bedlam,
Turned on the Doc, bit the hand that fed him.

And you, Dr. X, who killed by moonlight,
We loved your scream in the laboratory
When the panel slid and the night was starry
And you threw the inventor in the crocodile pit
(An obscure point: Did he deserve it?)
And you took the gold to Transylvania
Where no one guessed how insane you were.

We thank you for the moral and the mood,
Dear Dr. Cliché, Nurse Platitude.
When we meet again by the Overturned Grave,

[23]

Near the Sunken City of the Twisted Mind,
(In *The Son of the Son of Frankenstein*),
Make the blood flow, make the motive muddy:
There's a little death in every body.

PARTING AT THE ZOO

I saw two lovers separating where
Surrounding iron held their gift of sleep.
Wry leaves made dry distinctions in the air.
Twittering, the apes sang. Serpents paired.
The reservoir was still. A lion roared.

Do lovers looking in their eyes at night
See animals or friends? In these, eyesight
So blinded them they could distinguish neither:
They stood up bearing graves for each,
In mourning clothes, incapable of speech.

I saw a ruin growing in the park.
In opposite directions they walked then.
The evening blurred. The vista paled.
And everywhere I looked, I saw black, black
Rolling from the cages of the lovers' world.

That night in dreams, the animals sang
All love away. I saw the lion tear
Through hatred's cage of claw and fang
To spring at the throat of love. And now
That ruin in the park grows everywhere.

SKIN AND BONE

The wick burns down the length
Of its cold paraffin
Till the burned string's strength
Sputters, and is gone;

And if you have not seen
The spider in his web
Make of that silk machine
A jail where small things ebb,

You cannot know I mean
The skin around the bone.

The heavy leaves of blight
Curl inward and come down;
It is the moth of light
The darkness tumbles down;

And if you cannot see
The crab's dry rattling legs
Turn over, claw the sky,
And wither to the dregs,

You cannot know I mean
The skin around the bone.

The string stands for the nerve,
The web stands for the brain,
The wing for the eyelid's curve,
The leaf stands for the skin,

But the claw is appetite
That feeds on that heart each night
You cannot know. I mean
The skin around the bone.

MAINE

The days are clear as primitive paintings,
The twilight's fine as Japanese prints.
At night, only the ocean moves

As we drift out on purest dark,
Innocent as the winds of spring,
Old as the fossils in the rock.

CHALK FROM EDEN

Doctrine has wound of lovers' limbs
A sulphurous wreath of antonyms,
And strung its gnomes of hell and damn
On wiry thoughts throughout all time,
And taken a stick to the naked couple,
Cursing the moonlight, the river bend,
Music, and dark—and the world goes round.

For virgins will come, all green thumb,
Into the garden of their martyrdom,
And dilly-dally in the orchard air,
And say to holy doctrine, "Less we care
For the black commandments of your lasting scruple
Than we do for a dancer who is supple;
Hell is not heaven, and go to the devil."

Doctrine has turned pilgrims of pleasure
Into dull spinsters of meanest measure,
Made of pure angels infidels,
And hauled wet witches out of dry wells.

There is a warning in the steeple,
Spelling a lesson for good people,
Which leads us back to the garden's apple.

But time and again, in every season,
Love is a meeting mating reason,
And young and old walk in their park,
And spin in their skins from light to dark.
The sheets of time have a common wrinkle,
For youngsters will take their flaking chalk
And write of love on wall and sidewalk.

A BOX AT THE OPERA

(*For William Meredith*)

Into some country where sopranos
Beautifully rage and range, arranging
Echoes beyond the score's intention,
I watched you travel. All was hung there:
Ourselves buoyed up in a box by darkness,
The faint oval glitter across the theatre,
The stage suspended in a gilt rectangle.

Who is to know when music's angel
Arrests its flight and, whirring downward,
Stops to undo its gold illusion?
The music lovers gather at the bar,
The chandeliers assume their mimic brilliance,
The prompter disappears below the stage.

There must be something in old age
That seems like this: a theatre filled
With all that might and could not happen,

More an intermission than an ending,
The audience about to leave its seats,
The actors about to become less real.

And there is someone much too real,
Suffering somewhere in a theatre,
Unknown to the audience or performers,
Whose heart is about to break or stop,
Whose mind is about to close on music,
Whose eyes are about to close on love,

Whose single tear might cancel magic
(Even the magic about that tear),
The marble stairs be brimmed with panic,
The angel dead who brought the music,
And, out in the lobby, a white silk scarf
Hang in the wind like a lost love.

RAIN

Dear, on a day of dumb rain,
When cats sleep and trees grow,
And, outside the windowpane,
Imaginary fish flow,
We, as lovers, lace our arms
Securely round each other's back,
Hoping to stave off lightning's harm,
To counter thunder's crack.

Then pleasure is as easy as
The body's closeness, and the mind's;
There is a kind of love that has
Them separate, but body finds
Body too tasteless without thought,
And lovers feel, when face to face,
That mere intellect falls short,
Short of an embrace.

Dwindling, the slim rain makes us seem
As green as any world that grows;
Intransitive in sleep, we dream
Ourselves curled tightly as the rose,
Whose bud we cannot praise too much:
This is the start of every song
That no philosophy can touch—
And only the dead are wrong.

ROUNDS

I

Tented against the glare
Of sunlight overhead,
The leaves screen the heat,
And what might devil air
Angelically is bred,
By coolness and by fleet
Shutters everywhere,
To summer's true bed:
The greenness of retreat.

We follow freshness where
The spring winds led,
And climb to heaven's seat
Up an endless stair
To green rooms just ahead
On persevering feet;
Opening each door,
We find, refurbishèd,
New worlds complete.

How meagre was the spare
Landscape we have shed!
How rare the bird's sweet
Whistle, full and clear,
That sings of the unsaid
Above the green sheet
Spread to cover bare
Earth and the new dead!
Angelic and elite

Heiresses of air,
We feel you overhead,
And though we may not greet
You equally, our share
Is half the marriage bed
We come to on young feet
To wed you everywhere,
Our flesh no longer lead.
Lightly your wings beat.

II

Fire and leaf are kin
When the leaves blow away
And the bitter season reigns.
The sky erases green
From one more tree each day
Till only the pale stains
Of summers that have been
Fade in the sun's ray.
We make of these remains

A fire for within:
Blade after blade of hay,
Deserts of dry grains,
Are stored within the bin
Of the color-wheeling tree.
Astringent in our veins,
Thin life, a pricking pin,
Bleeds the summer lie
Only the blood retains.

Pinion and horizon
Rise on a changed day
When beasts of weathervanes,
Turning their burnt tin,
Spin against the sky.
Holding the long reins
That fire in the sun,
Flame, like a runaway,
Races the long rains

Whose seasonable din
Shatters the still day
Where false summer feigns
Old miracles of sun.
In mirrors of new gray,
The colorless remains
Of leaves, flame or green,
Hang or blow away
Till the kindling wanes.

III

The season of Alas
Winters in the sky;
The ground is white with snow.
What archeries of glass
Blind the naked eye,
Illusionary arrow!
Its target is a guess:
We aim at the bull's eye,
Half light, half shadow.

Draughtsmanship is less
Than color to the eye
In love with summer's show.
A season of duress
Paints a rare, wry
Canvas. Eyes that know
Shun the obvious:
There is no subtlety
Like white and its dumb-show.

A museum of undress,
What costumes it could try
It's happy to forego.
It is not sounding brass:
The bony and the spry
Plucked arpeggio
Can nakedly compress
Music to one sigh,
Mocking the piano.

Everything made less
Itself is winter's way:
The lowest trees bow low
To let the wind pass,
Rummaging the dry
Snow that sifts below
Their naked likenesses,
Cold as the cold sky,
Blind with heavy snow.

IV

Black and white go down.
Spring's petals spring,
One by one, to life;
Pink, or vermilion,
Upon the branch's sling
Is born and is brief.
A longing for the sun
Stretches along the limb
And hangs the shapely leaf.

A pink and green clown
Tumbles in the ring;
We see with disbelief
A comic in a gown
From sterile twigs wring
The greenest green sheaf
Of flowers under the sun,
And the sun itself strung
On flower and on leaf.

Now who can disown
The new-born changeling?
The woods and fields are rife
With grinning green;
And should the bee sting
Young flesh unsafe,
There's honey in the comb,
More honey coming
To tongues that have enough.

Angels, earth has shown
Its heart to be too big:
Standing in spring we sniff
A newness all our own,
And though its whirligig
Can spin us through one life,
And only one, on loan,
We dance a joyous jig
On limbs soon stiff.

UNDERWOOD

From the thin slats of the Venetian blinds
The sun has plucked a sudden metaphor:
A harp of light, reflected on the floor,
Disorients the chair and desk and door.
Those much too delicate hands still tapping
The Underwood seem now Hindu dancers
Or five or ten young Balinese children
Hopping up and down in a clearing where
The striped light scrapes through bamboo seedlings
And moves from skinny shade to thin veneer
And changes as the harp of light is changing
Its twanging image on the office floor,
Being so remarkably the blinding heir
Of something that is not, and yet is, there.

Once I watched at the water cooler
A face bent over the jet-thin water:
The iris of the bent eye changed its color
As if the water jet had stained it green;
I saw the animal head's slight shudder,

[44]

Lifted from the surface of that running stream.
Tall branches then grew green in the hallway,
Arching above a green-ferned pathway;
A screen of green leaves hung in the doorway.
Was that a mirror where I saw the beaked birds,
The sluggish coffin of the alligator,
The monkeys climbing up the sunlit tree trunks?
Or did imagination, in that corridor,
Create, like the harp, its sudden metaphor?

Inside that drawer, among the blotters, folders,
Memos, carbons, pencils, papers,
Is the youngest animal of all awaking
In that coarse nest where he's been sleeping?
If I should reach into that dangerous drawer,
What singular teeth might pierce my skin?
Or if he should leap, should I then kill him,
And watch, where the harp had set its lightness,
The marvellous animal blood go thin?

ASIDE BY THE SEASIDE

Your shallow skin, the skein of my concern,
Catches sea-summers in its undertows.
Blue rolling barrels from the ocean's floor
Shatter as thin as bridal furbelows.
   I am a swimmer at your shore,
    Though landing there, I drown the more.

All salty minds that sharpen on the sea
Are clearer for its movement and its sound.
The sun is speaking of a clarity
That none of us discovers underground.
   Stay close to me. Time must sever
    Us, far apart, or sleeping together.

SMALL ELEGY

In the smart room where Lennie lies,
French draperies are too silk for eyes
That like their hangings plain, like their ties
Thin-striped. Lennie will no more arise

And go now where the cocktail shakers shake
Their crystal energies and pianists fake
Some lovelorn valentines and, on the make,
Mirrored faces join, and part, and break.

And since those wretched limbs, not custom-made
But real, and common, in a last charade
Crumble into peace, who's to parade
Up Fifth and down with all his tricks of trade?

The chandelier, the chiffonier, the waste
By-products of the golden calf, Good Taste,
Surround his body. To his Never-Faced-
Reality, gentlemen, a final toast!

Damn it, he had good taste! That's all he had.
He knew the nearly-good from the not-quite-bad.
Lennie wore the first vest made of plaid.
Lennie gave it up when it became a fad.

Goodbye, Lennie—fad, plaid, and Madras!
May artificial angels and high brass
Proclaim a high-fidelity Mass
When you step from, and into glass.

LETTER TO AN IMAGINARY BRAZIL

(For Elizabeth Bishop)

The pink tongues of certain flowers having
Only colloquial names (they are
So tough they might be used for scouring)
Stick out suggestively among green pods,
And the green's tough, too, though it surprises
The fingernail that frees its milk from fibre,
Running a white thread down the hand. One plant's
No menace, but from the plane, one sees
A writhing settlement that hides its danger,
Where snake and puma wrestle on a floor
Of sliding vegetation, and the macaw
May tear a scale off as loud and brilliant
As any virtuoso bending over keys
Of black and white—those colors missing here,
Where all is earth-green, earth-red, earth-brown,
And a sulphurous yellow takes the breath
Away from the breather, Elizabeth.

[49]

The waterfall, cruel as a kind of love,
Which, because it moves, is forced to cut
Some life away, is still a version of
The pastoral by being beautiful:
A dynamo that distance turns to song.
The mountain, too, has its deception—
Imagined stillness, though explorers lie
Ironed out among its dark crevasses,
Where nature tries to wrest its forms from darkness:
Twisting, thickening spines and circles
Frightening the mind with a naturalism
That cannot weigh the difference between
A feather and a leaf. To fall asleep at night,
One thinks of nature as a human being:
The mountain a patriarch bending over life,
The waterfall a girl, stranded in a myth,
Whose tears have cut through rock, Elizabeth.

Though what is still may move, and come to grief,
Though what is moving stop, no longer safe,
I see you in your house upon a mountainside,
Lighting the lamps. When you look outside,
There is the room, hung up between the mountains,
Reflected on the other side of glass,

And, swinging in that double cage of light,
The mind flies out to objects of its love
And finds impenetrable forms and shapes
That you can formulate when you pin down
Each butterfly of thought upon your board.
You'll see, as fine as fern, a single tree
Which, sprouting all its foliage at once,
Will seem to move beneath a microscope
Until each cell is separate to the eye,
Thin-scaled as life upon the width of death,
Who cannot read your poems, Elizabeth.

THE TORTOISE-SHELL LORGNETTE

I have here a tortoise-shell
Lorgnette, beautifully made, but frail;
It has outlasted many kings.
Closed, one sees one speckled brown
Rectangle made of tinted glass;
Sprung open, two, and each is framed
By amber, brown, and shaded tan,
Bordered by tiny diamonds.
Seeming as light as air, it hangs
On a silk cord, also fine,
That twines around the wearer's neck
An almost imaginary line
Attached to the object by a clasp
So miniature as to seem abstract.
No museum piece, but made for use,
No glass showcase has ever been
Diminutive and delicate
Enough to mount this lorgnette in.

MODIFIED SONNETS

(Dedicated to adapters, condensers, and abridgers everywhere.)

SHALL I COMPARE THEE TO A SUMMER'S DAY?

Who says you're like one of the dog days?
You're nicer. And better.
Even in May, the weather can be gray,
And a summer sub-let doesn't last forever.
Sometimes the sun's too hot;
Sometimes it is not.
Who can stay young forever?
People break their necks or just drop dead!
But you? Never!
If there's just one condensed reader left
Who can figure out the abridged alphabet
    After you're dead and gone,
    In this poem you'll live on!

MUSIC TO HEAR, WHY HEAR'ST THOU MUSIC SADLY?

Why are you listening to the radio, crying?
The program's good. You're nice. What could be
    wrong?
If you don't like it, why don't you try dialling?
Why keep humming if you don't like the song?
You're tuned in to the best jazz, pop., and classical
The unions make. If you don't like 'em,
Try, they're not bad, just a bit nonsensical.
Or maybe it's that you'd like to be alone? H'mmn?
Listen, it's as good as Kostelanatz!
You know what tone he gets out of the strings.
They sound like a happy family. Honest.
Like when the kids sing what the mother sings.
    There's a lesson in it, though. Hear that tone?
    One person couldn't do it. Don't live alone!

WHEN IN DISGRACE WITH FORTUNE AND MEN'S EYES

When I'm out of cash and full of shame,
And crying to beat the band, alone,
And even God doesn't know my name,
And all I do is weep and moan,
I curse myself in the mirror,
Wishing I had a future,
Or some real pals, or was a good looker,
Or even a crazy artist or a deep thinker!
As I said, when even the old kicks seem tame,
And just when I hate myself the most,
I think about you. Then I'm o.k.
Just like a bird who hates the dirt
And can fly in the sky to get away.
    Thinking of you is as good as money.
    I'd give up royalties for you, honey.

AGAINST THAT TIME, IF EVER
THAT TIME COME

I hope I never live to see the day
When all you do is criticize my faults,
When maybe love's veil is torn away
And you don't think as much of me as you thought.
It's possible someday you'll pass me by
Without so much as a nod,
When the flame is low that used to be high,
Or maybe, even, dead!
Well, to make sure, I'm staying in,
Because, to tell the truth, I have some faults,
And I'm trying to develop my good side
So I won't have so much on that day to hide.
   If you threw me over, you wouldn't be far wrong;
   Who knows why lovers, like dogies, get along?

LOCAL PLACES

The song you sang you will not sing again,
Floating in the spring to all your local places,
Lured by archaic senses to the wood
To watch the frog jump from the mossy rock,
To listen to the stream's small talk at dark,
Or to feel the springy pine-floor where you walk—
If your green secrecies were such as these,
The mystery is now in other trees.

If, in the desert, where the cactus dryly,
Leniently allows its classic bloom
To perfume aridness, you searched for water,
And saw, at night, the scalp of sand begin
To ripple like the sea, as though the moon
Had tides to time those waves of light's illusion,
The rock that spilled so softly from your hand
Is now ten thousand other grains of sand.

If you lay down beside the breathing ocean,
Whose lung is never still, whose motion pulls

z

[57]

A night-net over sleep, you knew the way
It lulled the dreamer toward his vision, how
Drowned mariners turned over in its slough,
Green-eyed among the weeds. You see it now
A less than visionary sea, and feel
Only its blue surfaces were ever real.

Or if you were born to naked flatness
Of rock, or rock that twisted up in mountains,
The jagged risers stonily ascending,
And bent down once to see the mica's tight,
Flat scales of silver, layered in the granite,
And kept one scale to be your jewel at night,
Another sliver now breaks light; its gleam
Is similar to yours, yet not the same.

Once history has used your single name,
Your face is one time will not see again.
Into such a din is every singer born,
The general music mutes the single horn.
The lights in the small houses, one by one,
Go out, foundations topple slowly down—
The tree, the sand, the water, and the stone,
What songs they sing they always sing again.

THE PEACOCK

After we had wintered on the sparrow's meek
And ordinary music, we desired
The peacock's cry and iridescent eye,
Some untamed image that the mind might seek
To take it out of winter and restore
The summer wilderness it knew before.

Even in snow, we saw the peacock
Dance its passion in the wintry light.
Setting traps for the petty sparrow,
Mocking sparrow in the name of peacock,
We fed on a pleasure that the future knew,
Not knowing, then, what bird it was we slew.

Many winters since, the snow's white lead
Has thinned on the doorstep, disarmed the trees,
And snuffed the world out. The sparrows still
Chirp on their prosperous boughs. And yet,
The peacock will not lift its gifted head
Or wake in imagination's waiting bed.

TRAGEDY

Does a tear fall from the eye
When, falling from great heights,
The body usurps the sky
To die of its appetites?
Do the limbs seek the land
And the lungs a last song
When, burned by cruel wind,
They hurtle headlong?

When to that centre hurled,
Kings have far to fall—
So high, they see the world
Smooth as a round ball—
Perspective takes their wit,
And sceptre, crown, and ring
Must somersault to it,
The whole world darkening.

Those falls from pinnacles
Through miles of royal air

Turn widely in their wheels—
Beggar and priest are there.
All flights of steps may lead
To terror at the top,
The heart begin to bleed
Suddenly without stop,

As when old Caesar's whore
Tore Egypt from her skull,
Or Hamlet's Elsinore
Broke for a lack of will,
Or King Lear on his heath
Invoked the end of breath,
And fools fell out of myth
Into a real death.

All saviors of the city
Are lit by an unknown star;
Love, terror, pity
Walk where they are.
The kings of our great ills
Are dead, yet come to mind
When we fall from small hills
Into the common ground.

A SWIMMER IN THE AIR

That sea we see of surfaces
  Turned upside down would be another world:
A bone shop, soaked in pearl, a dumping-
Ground for rarities, the sea-maws pumping
    Grecian garbage Roman cities hurled
      Seaward westward toward our faces.

That sea would yield up secret farms,
  Gray-rotted by itself, encrusted thick
With unimaginable wealth, the spoil
Of deaf-mute drownings, the immemorial
    Dead, floating in a blue-green bailiwick
      Of nun-like plants, waving arms.

That sea will not turn over. See
  In its deepest keep, far from its shallow,
The formal, hidden iceberg, slant, oblique
With pregnancy below, thrust up its peak—
    Like ourselves in the water-beasted wallow,
      Caught in a cellular ecstasy.

In the same vein, all flesh conceals
   Articulation's fishnet, whose thread-bones
(A metaphysic harp from sky to heel)
Hang in the flesh that dangles from the creel
   Depending from the weedy Hand that owns
      All fishnets and all fishing reels.

His answers breed a further question:
   The fingernails of scale a snake will shed
In spring, coil after coil, on moistened clay,
Though similar to the serpent, wriggling away,
   Are but facsimiles, though not quite dead.
      Testing this, see how the rest shun

Drying memorials to that race
   That mined our viewpoint in the Garden,
Whose inching tape maneuvred in the sun
To measure every guilty length of Eden.
   Man is an animal that needs a warden
      To frighten off the Master's face,

For even an idiot sees a world
   No tree or dog would dream of, finds a name
For pain or absence of it, marries love

[63]

Of one kind or another. In his grove,
   Insensible fruit trees and wild game
      Grow naturally, though he lies curled,

     The spit and image of our wish,
    Smoking a pipe, with an ice-cold Cola
Clutched in one hand, and the Sunday funnies spread
On both his knees. He'll leave his lurching bed
    To throw hot jazz on an old victrola—
      A far cry from the primal fish

     Whose fine-boned spine our back remembers:
    The river bottoms, and the sea-silt soft
As soup, the mudflats where night crawlers came,
Tempted by the water tops to change the lame
    Arrangements, making of the air a loft
      Fitted to our brackish members,

     And out we clambered, eyeing land,
    Our moist eyes focused on the moron green,
Hot on our backs abnormal dryness, shadow
Forming in the seanets, seaweed into meadow,
    Finally landing at the foot of pine,
      Heavy with salty contraband

While the birds beautifully beat blue
  On erect wings, as magically they soared,
Feathered and efficient, from tallest trees to stake
A claim so ravishing that now we undertake
  To map an area we once ignored,
    Still exiles from that upper view,

    For, mummers of the ocean's Word,
  Our dry translations tidied from the deep,
Bespeak its ancient languages. The salt
Our tears and blood must harbor from its vault
  Is shed on every beach-head where we creep,
    Part man, dry fish, and wingless bird.

BOILING EGGS

My waking hunger wants its hourglass
Turned upside down to clock my boiling eggs.
  Bobbing about, they've lost their sea legs,
   And though no theorem of Pythagoras,
    Prove, by that stately 8,
That even early birds can be too late,
For appetite requires that these yet unborn
Chicks give up the ghost this wintry morn.

One more minute now. How I regret (poor chicks!)
To take them out of Nature so that I may dine.
  Theirs is a fate that my arithmetic's
   Not wholly to be blamed for—the Great Design,
    Mother Nature, not my clock,
Prescribes for hens the ardor of the cock—
Some learn, from experience, how one good egg
Can scramble up a lifetime. Were I to renege,

Ponder still their ends: cock or hen,
(Or worse, a capon), at the finish line

Meets a grisly doom. Who's to say when
They'd vanish dimly down the throats of men?
    The end cannot be breached:
For whether eggs are coddled, baked, or poached,
Or Benedict, or fried, or served Foo Yung,
They make a tasty morsel for the tongue.

They're done. I put them in a tablespoon,
One by one, beneath the water tap
    To cool, and when I break the lime cocoon,
    The membrane curls away, a tattered map.
      Mingled in a cup,
Buttered, salted, peppered, I scoop them up,
Who are not what they were. Now they're uncased,
I cannot tell a lie: I like the taste.

The hourglass, standing on my pantry shelf,
Immune to both my hunger and their state,
    Diurnally is fated to reverse itself
    And time two boiling eggs at the exact same rate.
      Satiety can't last:
The ultimate in feasts leads to a new repast—
Tomorrow when my hourglass is turned about,
Appetite will dine again, and time run out.

III

A WINTER COME

I

When frost moves fast and gardens lose their ground
And gold goes downward in the trees, no sound
Accompanies departures of the leaves,
Except when the wind hurtles into air
Dead shapes the coming winter will inter;
Then the thinnest music starts to stir
A faint, crisp scraping in the startled ear:
The leaves that feed the new leaves of next year.

II

Branch of a being that is bent by snow,
How many birds desert your stiffened bough?
There was a cage of lyrics in the air,
A bird for every leaf suspended there,
Who chirped at sunlight in the foliage
That farmed its summer at the meadow's edge;
And now an arm as thin as any wing
Rasps the iron air, bereft of song.

III

A child lay down in his imagined grave
To see the form he'd make engraved in snow,
But even that feigned hollow filled with snow;
And, rising on a landscape blurred a bit
By shadows of an adumbrated blue,
He came upon two worlds he had not known:
One was his being, one his mind let go
Until the light would take the blue from snow.

IV

Your breath precedes you on a winter's day,
An insubstantial cloud, as if to say,
All solid things are blown to vapor soon.
Look up! The scimitar of the moon
Is but a remnant of the round it was,
Is but a ringlet of the ring to be,
As, riding forth, the breath that marked your birth
Will have its heir, before it comes to death.

V

As birds come nearer for a crust of bread
Across the frozen snow, by hunger led
To stamp fine footprints on a scroll of white,
So winter is a world where appetite
Grows bolder by necessity, where the fox
Betrays his fable, and the cold unlocks
Stiff beggars from the doorways. Time grows old
In the knuckles of an old man blue with cold.

VI

The racing waterfall that slowed in fall
Has thinned to a trickle or an icicle
And stands as quiet as the rocks it willed
To move. As though expecting it to fall,
A listener stands upon a rim of silence,
Seeing a changed world prepared to change,
The waterfall silent on its breakneck shelf,
And silence a spectacle in itself.

VII

Adrift upon thin ice before he falls
Asleep is the sleeper deep in snow
That falls in imaginary winters in
The mind remembering the snow when no
Snow is falling, who will raise a blind,
Certain he has sensed its slow descent,
And find the crippled world he left behind,
And his transfiguration in the mind.

VIII

Those statues, born long after funerals
Have mourned their subjects, stand in every park—
Stone statesmen stiff upon their pedestals,
Who dominate indifferent day and dark.
Blind to all the cruder jokes of snow,
A socket of sheer cold behind each eye,
They cannot know that even sculptors go
Where all the celebrated sitters lie.

IX

Who reads by starlight knows what fire is,
The end of words, and how its mysteries
Go running in the flame too quick to see,
As language has a light too bright to be
Mere fact or fiction. By ambiguity
We make of flame a word that flame can burn,
And of love a stillness, though the world can turn
On its moment, and be still. Or turn and turn.

X

And what of love that old men dead and gone
Have wintered through, and written messages
In snow so travellers, who come too warm
To what may grow too cold, be safe from harm?
They know the fire of flesh is winter's cheat
And how the icy wind makes young blood sweet
In joining joy, which age can never have.
And that is what all old men know of love.